# GHOST TRAIN

# Ghost Train

## Matt Borczon

Ghost Train
Matt Borczon

© 2016 Matt Borczon

ISBN-13: 978-0-9983373-7-1

Weasel Press
Manvel, TX
www.weaselpress.com

Interior: Weasel
Typeset: Palatino Linotype

Printed in the U.S.A.

# Table of Contents

# GHOST TRAIN

# Good bye

The first
time I
left for
Fort Jackson
Mark's girlfriend
was crying
so hard
you'd think
it was him
going instead
of me
and I
remember
you were
pissed that
she was
there since
we left
the kids
at home
so I
could just
leave fast
break clean
hopefully be
on the
plane before
reality set
in but
instead she

cried like
a baby
or the
manic depressive
she was
while I
shifted
uncomfortably
from foot
to foot
not sure
what to
say to
 you and
less sure
what you
should say
to me
good bye
seemed too
thin but
now I
wish I
would have
said it
considering
how much
of me
never made
it home.

## Skin

I didn't
understand
why when
that soldier
broke and
just shut
down stopped
eating or
drinking
just curled
up like a
sick cat
until they
took him
to Germany
the army
would not
let him
wear his
uniform
 home
instead
they left
it like
snake skin
stinking  of
fear  and
piss on
that sterile
hospital floor

## Marines

Had to
sit guard
duty
on any
body they
shot but
did not
kill
had to
stay at
their bed
until
the detainees
were well
enough to
leave the
hospital
or died
from their
wounds
most of
them would
ask us
corpsmen
if we
knew where
they could
find an
extra bullet
to finish
the job.

# Ghost train

On my
worst day
six soldiers
died in
one twelve
hour shift
some in
the ward
others on
the operating
table
I think
maybe
everyone
did everything
right and
it still
all went
so wrong
but by
that time
I was
no longer
sure what
right even
felt like
and wrong
was pouring
out of
every body

bag hiding
in every
patient bed
and riding
me like
an ass
or second
skin as
I moved
from one
person to
the next
with no
 time
to question
my decisions
only time
to act
so their
deaths
sat inside
me  like an
unexploded
bomb with
a slow
burning fuse
it took
years before
it went
off releasing
sad ghosts
that  now

want
the answer
to questions
I never
had time
to ask
that now
hold
my nightmares
as  their
personal
playground
their hornets
nest their
private property
blank canvas
empty pocket
and
slow train
they ride
 in
forever.

## End of shift

The Afghan
soldier was
shot in
the chest
and thigh
mostly I
just held
his arms
down while
they put
in a
central line
and the
Lieutenant
hung bag
after bag
of blood
there were
6 people
working on
him and
he seemed
stable as
we sent
him into
the OR
that night
lieutenant
told me
he had

died on
the operating
table we
could not
keep enough
blood in
him he
said just
before walking
away funny
I really
thought he
was going
to be
OK he
said over
his shoulder
I thought
so too
but back
then I
think I
thought  the
same thing
about the
Lieutenant
and me.

## Human resources

Spent 7
days in
HR working
on files
and charts
I thought
it would
be a
nice change
of pace
from the
ward and
the blood
and bandages
just a
long row
of cabinets
and I
only worked
day shift
that week
but after
the 31$^{st}$
death certificate
I filed
into skinny
folders
I knew
for certain
that death

was everywhere
here and
it reduced
everyone's  life
to 10
pages or
less.

## Survival kit

In place
of medication
try prayer
tears strong
drink true
love or
anything
you can
wrap your
arms and
legs around
try lies
try truth
try saint
johns wart
try talking
to a
therapist
try talking
to nobody
try keeping
your ghosts
inside
your head
they are
already
inside your
nightmares
and they
rule there
use long
sleeves and

dark socks
to cover
scars that
show and
a large
glass jar
to hold
the scars
that don't
show screw
the lid
down tight
and bury
it out
in your
victory garden
but for
Christ's  sake
try something
fight
if not
to win
at least
for keeps.

## A kind person

in Kuwait
2 weeks
from home
I hear
the word
compassion
fatigue for
the first
time in
my life

after all
you have
seen you
may just
be too
tired
to care
about people
for awhile

we were
advised to
sleep a
lot and
watch movies
decompress
before we
head home
and remember

you may
not be
able to
be a
kind person
for awhile

5 years
later and
I am still
not a
kind person

not any
kind of
person.

## Post deployment

I stripped
and cleaned
both my
rifle and
9mm and
gave back
my body
armor and
two full
sea bags
felt a
hundred pounds
lighter for
awhile as
I walked
around Norfolk
trying to
feel like
a civilian again

I remember
really enjoying
those first
few weeks
back home
before the
weight
of everything
I could
not give

back from
the war
hit me
and I
crushed
everyone
those I
loved and
those I
barely knew.

## Gestalt

My friend
Anita told
me that
after loosing
both parents
in a
horrible
car wreck
she struggled
with even
going outdoors
she was
hyper vigilant
with her
2 young
children and
felt like
her life
was falling
in on
itself
she had
been a
psych major
and spent
time at
the Gestalt
institute
these ideas
helped her

get past
her pain
so she
suggested
I imagine
a white
room where
I go
to hold
and comfort
my most
beloved
my wife
kids and
my dead
father
then I
comfort
the people
I only
knew a
short time
soldiers
Afghan children
or even
strangers
then I
hold and
comfort my
enemies
the boy
who beat

me up
on the
playground
girls who
stole my
heart and
fucked my
friends
then I
am supposed
to imagine
offering comfort
to the
one who
hurt me
the most
only I
can not
imagine who
that is

me in
2010 before
the war
or me
in 2015
still unable
to let
it all
go.

# Repressed memories

Come to
me in
dreams
crawling out
from under
aquacel  dressings
I packed
into soldiers
wounds
they spit
at me
from inside
colostomy bags
as I
empty them
or cry
out in
the voices
of dead
infants
on windless
nights
there are
as many
memories
as dead
soldiers
as limbs
blown off
as children

who stepped
on IED's
and dissolved
into a
thin red
sigh
they are
real and
as painful
as
the arthritis
In my
hips that
make  it
so hard
to walk
as I
try to
carry these
 coffin
sized memories
that I
am not
able
to put
down.

## Who Am I

What good
is there
in bleeding
all over
everyone
with these
stories of
amputated
women and
broken soldiers
who am
I to
spread these
nightmares
outside of
my own
head
I already
wake my
children with
my screams
at night
and scare
my wife
with my
silence and
frustrate
my psychiatrist
by refusing
pills so

who am
I to
speak about
things a
man should
want to
forget.

I am
another broken
American promise
poor working
class middle
aged man
who fell
for a
Roy Rodgers
John Wayne
line of
sands of
Iwo Jima
smoke screen
who packed
the wounds
and cleaned
the dead
who pulled
the staples
from human
stumps and
swept bone
fragments into

small piles
I'm the
guy who
had to
hold it
together until
I could
lose it
all in
night terrors
and dead
baby dreams
who still
looks for
survivors in
crowded bars
and restaurants
I am
the proverbial
poor boy
who fought
a rich
mans war
and I
am what's
left
after you
raise what's
left
of the flag.

# Fall in

Behind the
dead soldiers
fall in
behind the
children crushed
or shot
or burned
beyond recognition
fall in
behind the
local nationals
and their
wives blown
open farther
than we
could sew
closed
fall in
behind my
old friend
who was
eaten by
cancer and
was more
dead than
alive before
he even
knew
fall in
and throw

blood against
my dreams
fall in
to
graft skin
over the
hole in
side of
me that
used to
hold my
faith and
hope and
carry my
bones like
rifles as
you all
 take
the long
march through
the rest
of my
life.

## Explaining Afghanistan to a 7 year old.

If it
was a
nursery rhyme
I would
tell you
that I
was not
the egg
who had
a great
fall but
I was
one of
the kings
horses or
one of
the kings
men who
could not
put him
back together
again so
my eyes
were filled
with tears
and my
hands covered
in yolk

when I
came home
with egg
on my
face and
no country
to call
my own.

## PTSD 4

Dump the
sand from
your boots
and check
for camel
spiders
remember to
get your
uniform from
the laundry
pay the
extra dollar
so they
get the
blood off
of it
make sure
your mopp
gear is
under your
rack because
its late
and if
you manage
to fall
asleep
you are
sure to
need it
knowing where

your nightmares
are headed.

## burn

I wish
I could
just call
my ghosts
to attention
and they
 would
fall in
holding their
body parts
and bandages
my regrets
and nightmares
like rifles
or children
waiting for
me to
march them
route step
to the
edge of
the world
where I
would light
a match
and watch
those fuckers
burn
cause it
took me 10

months to
get out
of Afghanistan
and its
been 4
years and
I'm still
no closer
to home.

## PTSD 8

My muse
is a
severed
leg that
 I find
in my
bed
in every
single
nightmare
I've had
since the
war.

## PTSD 9

If you
stick your
arm in
 up to
 the elbow
inside  the
hornets
nest that
is my
life
you will
only feel
the wind

and only
hear the
war.

## Frozen Charlotte

was a
Victorian-era
doll that
slept in
a coffin
and was
baked into
cakes for
children
a reference
to what
can happen
when you
don't listen
to your
parents the
story is
based on
a girl
who froze
to death
in an
open sleigh
one winters
night

I am
not sure
why this
piece of

information
sticks with
me except
that since
Afghanistan
I
have also
found pale
dead children
and soldiers
with or
without coffins
in my food
and in
my bed

nightmares
reminding
me of
the cost
of a
war
never won
never over
never gone

## New Year 2016

after the
ball drops
and my
brain closes
down the
last neurons
with vodka
blue misery
and white
noise
I woke
late to
the realization
that the
changes in
me that
scare my
mom and
sadden my
brother are
not gone
I have
not managed
again this
year
to turn
back into
what they
all expected
and found

easier to
love
so I
begin 2016
still working
my way
through the
ward of
that hospital
in the
bloody mouth
of that
war now
over for
five years
only the
faces will
 change

there will
be new
recruits arriving
shot bleeding
and blown
to red
pieces
 tonight and
every night
in my
dreams

## Sounds

my wife
says her
favorite
sound is
the squeak
of sneakers
on a
basketball
court

my son
says its
the click
and hum
of turning
on his
guitar amplifier

my daughter
loves the
sound of
babies laughing
or sleeping
equally

when asked
I always
say I
like the
sound of

nothing

its easier
than trying
to explain
that after
almost 5
years I
still hear
the sound
of screaming
soldiers and
detainees

the hum
of suction
pumps and
wound vacs

the rumble
of helicopters
and artillery
near and
far away

the screams
of children
crying in
pain at
the loss
of their
families

I hear
this
on city
street in
empty rooms
everywhere
every day
awake and
in my
dreams

so I
long for
the absolute
quiet that
so far
I can
only find
at the
bottom of
my whiskey
bottle or
at the
maximum
dose of
my medication
and it
is so
elusive as
to be
imaginary

not half
as real
as these
sounds of
a war
I am
still fighting
inside my
self
day after
day.

## Add it up

2,268
Coalition
and local
National patients
passed through
the hospital
I served
in during
my time
in Afghanistan

that's how
many decades
of a
rosary
how many
turns of
a prayer
wheel
how many
Buddhist chants
or Christian
prayers

how many
burning
poppy fields
how many
rounds of
ammunition

how many
missing limbs
or dead
children
how many
detainees
and young
soldiers

how many
crying wives
and long
distance
phone calls
how many
missed
birthdays and
lonely holidays

how many
miles of
ground taken
and how
many miles
lost
how many
IEDS exploded
and how
many left
for people
to still
find

how many
therapy sessions
and psych
medications
how many
nightmares
and how
 many
years will
I lose
 adding
it all
up and
hoping its
sum is
more than
everything
I 've lost
since coming
home.

Some of these poems have appeared in

*Red Efts*
*Dead snakes*
*Yellow chair review*
*Rasputin*
*Dissident Voice*
*Anti Heroin Chic*
*Unscooped Bagel*
*Revolution John*
*the Hobo Camp Review*

Matthew Borczon is a writer and Navy sailor from Erie Pa, his book *A Clock of human Bones* won the Yellowchair reviews chap book contest in 2015. His work has appeared in many online and print journals including Red efts, dissident voice, dead snakes, big hammer, anti heroin chic, drunk in a midnight choir, the beatnik cowboy and others. He is married with 4 children and 3 jobs. Life keeps him very busy.

Out Now with Weasel Press

*Miffed and Peeved in the U.K.* by Neil S. Reddy

*Harmonious Anarchy* by Matthew David Campbell

*The Seven Yards of Sorrow* by David E. Cowen

*Wayward Realm* by Sendokidu "the fox" Adomi

*Uhaul* by Emily Ramser

*Exist in the Moon* by Jessi Schultz

*Dormant Volcano* by Ken Jones

*Evergreen* by Sarah Frances Moran

*Rising from the Ashes* by Mason O'Hern

*the first breath you take after you give up* by michael prihoda

*In and Of Blood* by Kat Lewis

*Everybody But You* by Thia Sexton

*Civilized Beasts*

*Vagabonds: Anthology of the Mad Ones*

*Degenerates: Voices for Peace*

*The Haunted Traveler*

*Satan's Sweethearts* by Marge Simon & Mary Turzillo

Coming Soon to Weasel Press

*Night at the End of the Tunnel* by Mark Greenside

*Taxi Sam* by Neil S. Reddy

*Wine Country* by Robin Wyatt Dunn

*I Am a Terrorist* by Sarah Frances Moran

*Thirsty Earth* by Chris Wise

*How Well You Walk Through Madness*